# How to use this book

## 1 Cut each page from the book.

Then cut along the T-shaped line to separate each section of the page so it is easier for your child to handle the pieces.

This book is structured so your child will advance gradually from easy to challenging activities. The activities are arranged according to difficulty based on the number of parts, the different sizes and shapes of the parts, and the amount of folding. We encourage your child to complete the activities in the order presented. However, it is okay to create whichever craft your child likes as long as he or she is capable of completing it.

## 2 Cut the parts, then paste them on the base.

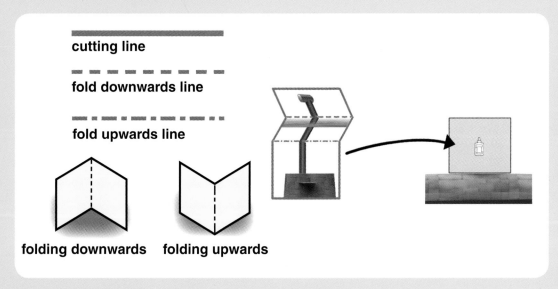

cutting line

fold downwards line

fold upwards line

folding downwards      folding upwards

If your child has difficulty cutting or pasting, it is okay for you to help.

## 3 Play with the completed crafts.

When your child has completed a craft, please offer him or her lots of praise. Furthermore, please encourage your child to play with the craft and have fun.

Try to limit the number of pages your child will complete in a day. It is best to end the day's activity when your child still wants to do more.

You may also want to bind the completed crafts together like a book, or connect them like a poster. Your child may want to continue playing with his or her completed crafts and share them with others.

# How to choose and hold scissors

Scissors can be dangerous if not handled properly. Keep an eye on your child when he or she is doing the cutting exercises.

## How to choose a good pair of scissors

1. Choose safety scissors with round tips.

2. Choose scissors with holes that suit your child's hands and fingers.

3. Choose scissors your child can open and close easily.

▲ Please choose easy-to-use safety scissors. Pictured on the right are plastic safety scissors.

## How to cut with scissors

Show your child how to put his or her thumb into the smaller hole and his or her forefinger and middle finger into the bigger hole of the scissors. If the bigger hole is large enough, have your child put his or her ring finger into the hole as well.

When your child holds scissors, please align his or her hand with the scissors so that they form a straight line when viewed from above.

▲ Please try to align your child's hand with the scissors so that they form a straight line.

# How to choose glue and how to paste

If your child will be using glue for the first time, carefully select a type of glue that he or she will enjoy using.

Please choose a child-safe product in an easy-to-use container. Your child can use a glue stick but it is best for children to use glue that can be applied by hand. Children enjoy the tactile experience of spreading glue with their fingers.

▲ Please choose child-safe glue.

**Tips for pasting**

Line your table with scrap paper before your child starts. Have your child apply an appropriate amount of glue onto the tip of his or her middle finger and then spread it thinly on the part to be pasted. Please put the glue on the side with the glue symbol.

When your child is applying glue, encourage him or her to hold the part with one hand and apply the glue onto it with the other. This is difficult for young children, you can hold the paper for your child at first.

▲ Begin by placing glue onto the part. Then ask your child to use his or her finger to spread the glue on the designated area.

# 1 Fire Engine

Cut and fold the water, then paste it on the base to complete.
Play with the water from the fire engine to make it put out the fire.

HOW TO CREATE AND PLAY

1. Cut along ▬▬▬.
Then fold downwards along ▬ ▬ ▬.

2. Paste the part on the base.

3. Move the part to make the water put out the fire.

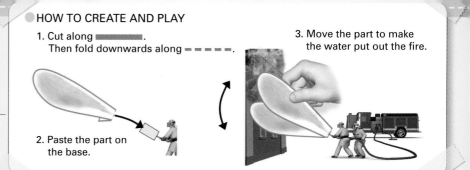

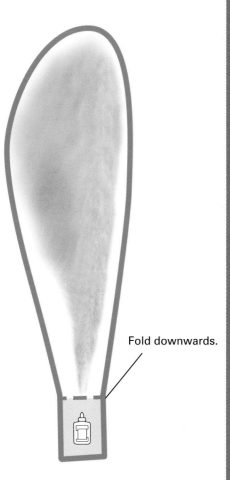

Fold downwards.

## Fire Engine

A fire engine puts out fires by spraying water.

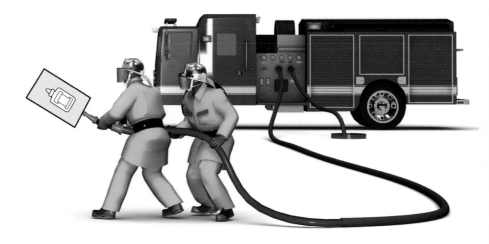

# 2 Bookmobile

■ Cut and fold the bookmobile hatch, then paste it on the base to complete.
Play with the bookmobile to make it open the bookshelf.

● HOW TO CREATE AND PLAY

1. Cut along ▬▬▬.
   Then fold upwards along ━ ·· ━ ·· ━.

2. Paste the part on the base.

3. Move the part to make the bookmobile open the bookshelf.

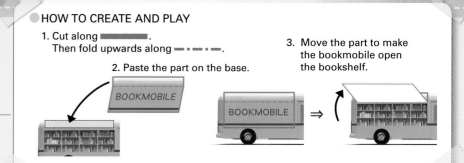

## Bookmobile

A bookmobile lends books to people who live far from a library.

BOOKMOBILE

Glue the back.

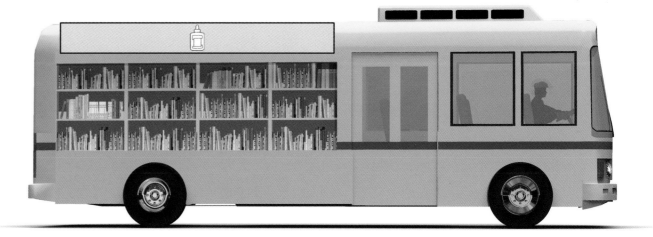

# 3 Snow Blower

■ Cut and fold the snow, then paste it on the base to complete.
Play with the snow blower to make it shoot the snow away.

● HOW TO CREATE AND PLAY

1. Cut along ▬▬▬▬▬.
   Then fold downwards along – – – – –.

3. Move the part to make the snow blower blow the snow away.

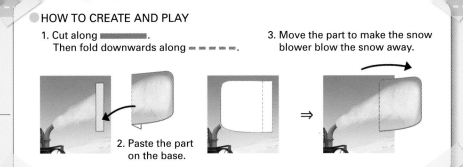

2. Paste the part on the base.

## Snow Blower

A snow blower picks up snow on the road and blows it away.

# 4 Submarine

● HOW TO CREATE AND PLAY

1. Cut along ▭▭▭▭.
   Then fold downwards along ‑ ‑ ‑ ‑ ‑
   and upwards along ‑ ∙ ‑ ∙ ‑.

2. Paste the part on the base.

3. Move the part to make the periscope rise above the sea for a look around.

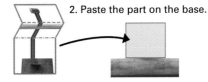
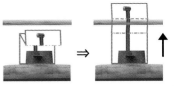

■ Cut and fold the periscope, then paste it on the base to complete.
Play with the periscope to make it rise above the sea for a look around.

## Submarine

A submarine extends a periscope above the sea to see the surroundings.

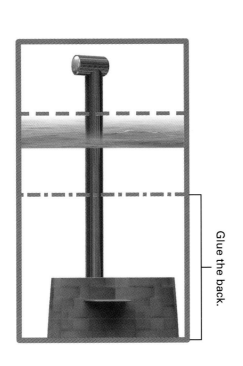

Glue the back.

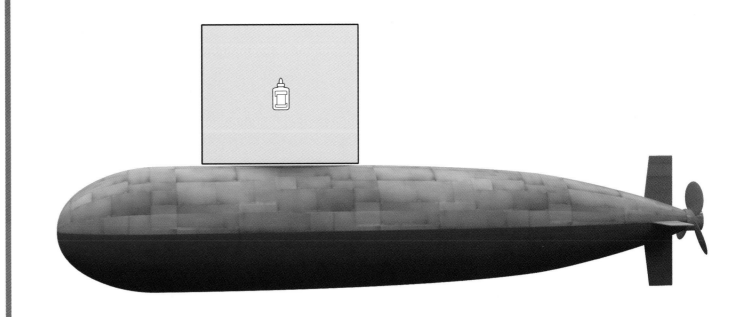

# 5 Truck

■ Cut and fold the cargo hatch, then paste it on the base to complete.
Play with the truck to make it open and close the cargo hatch.

● HOW TO CREATE AND PLAY

1. Cut along ▬▬▬▬.
   Then fold downwards along ━ ━ ━ ━
   and upwards along ━·━·━·━.

2. Paste the part on the base.

3. Move the part to make the truck open and close the cargo hatch.

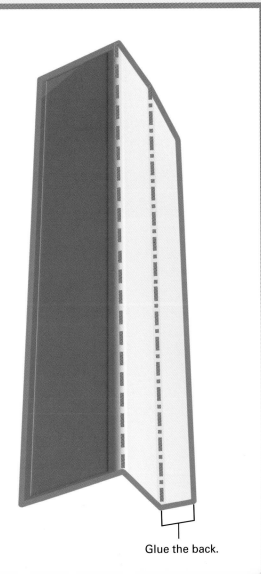

Glue the back.

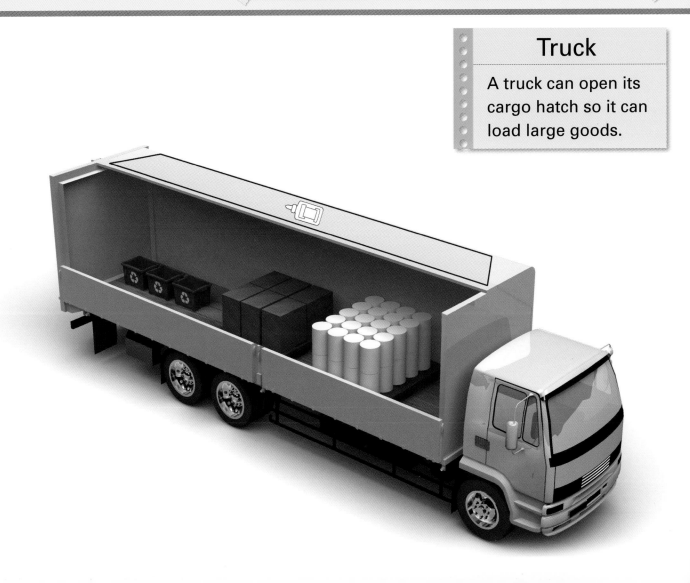

## Truck

A truck can open its cargo hatch so it can load large goods.

# 6

# Hot Air Balloon

■ Cut and fold the balloon, then paste it on the base to complete.
Play with the hot air balloon to make it rise into the sky.

● HOW TO CREATE AND PLAY

1. Cut along ▬▬▬▬.
   Then fold downwards along ▬ ▬ ▬ ▬
   and upwards along ▬ ▪ ▬ ▪ ▬.

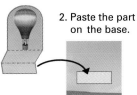

2. Paste the part on the base.

3. Move the part to make the hot air balloon rise into the sky.

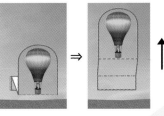

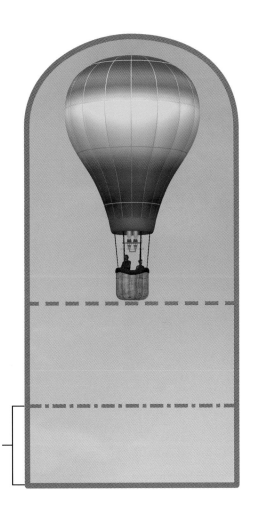

Glue the back.

## Hot Air Balloon

A hot air balloon rises by heating the air inside the balloon.

# 7 Rocket

■ Cut and fold the rocket, then paste it on the base to complete.
Play with the rocket to make it launch.

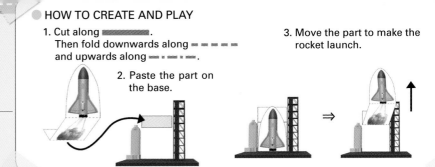

**HOW TO CREATE AND PLAY**

1. Cut along ▬▬▬.
   Then fold downwards along – – – –
   and upwards along –·–·–·–.

2. Paste the part on the base.

3. Move the part to make the rocket launch.

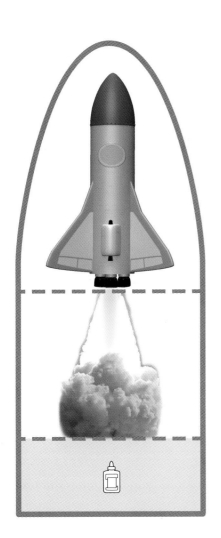

## Rocket

A rocket launches satellites, spaceships and more.

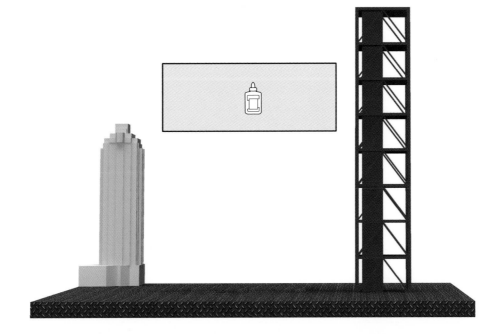

# 8 Hydrofoil

■ Cut and fold the hydrofoil, then paste it on the base to complete.
Play with the hydrofoil to make it lift onto the water's surface.

● HOW TO CREATE AND PLAY

1. Cut along ▬▬▬.
Then fold downwards along ▬ ▬ ▬ ▬
and upwards along ▬ · ▬ · ▬.

2. Paste the part on the base.

3. Move the part to make the hydrofoil lift onto the water's surface.

Glue the back.

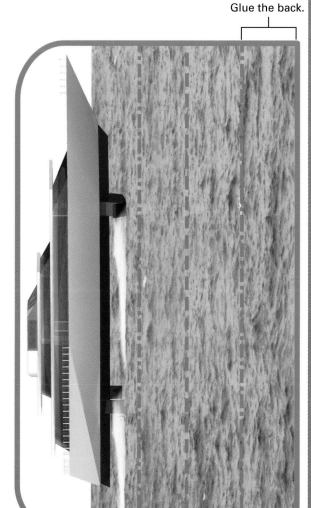

## Hydrofoil

The body of the hydrofoil lifts out of the water onto wing-like supports when moving forward.

# 9 Crane Truck

■ Cut and fold the load, then paste it on the base to complete.
Play with the crane truck to make it lift the load.

● HOW TO CREATE AND PLAY

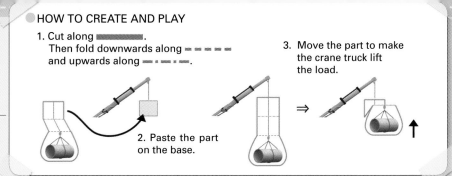

1. Cut along ▬▬▬.
   Then fold downwards along ▬ ▬ ▬
   and upwards along ▬ · ▬ · ▬.

2. Paste the part on the base.

3. Move the part to make the crane truck lift the load.

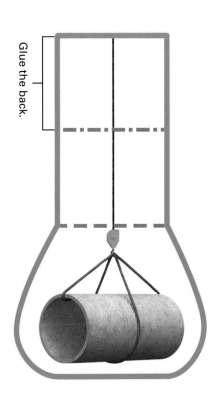

Glue the back.

## Crane Truck

A crane truck can lift and move heavy loads.

# 10 Backhoe

■ Cut and fold the arm of the backhoe, then paste it on the base to complete.
Play with the backhoe to make it dig a hole in the ground.

● HOW TO CREATE AND PLAY

1. Cut along ▬▬▬.
   Then fold downwards along ▬ ▬ ▬ ▬
   and upwards along ▬ ▪ ▬ ▪ ▬.

2. Paste the part on the base.

3. Move the part to make the backhoe dig a hole in the ground.

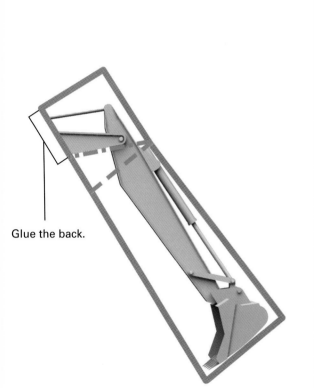

Glue the back.

## Backhoe

A backhoe digs holes in the ground at construction sites.

# Helicopter

■ Cut, fold and paste the helicopter, then paste the part on the base to complete.  Play with the helicopter to make it fly.

● HOW TO CREATE AND PLAY

1. Cut along ▭▭▭.
   Then fold downwards along ▬ ▬ ▬
   and upwards along ▬ · ▬ · ▬.

2. Glue the backs together.

3. Paste the part on the base.

4. Move the part to make the helicopter fly.

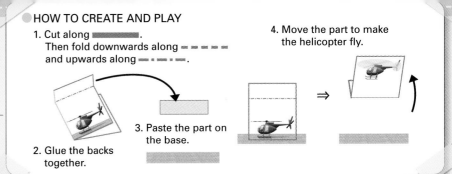

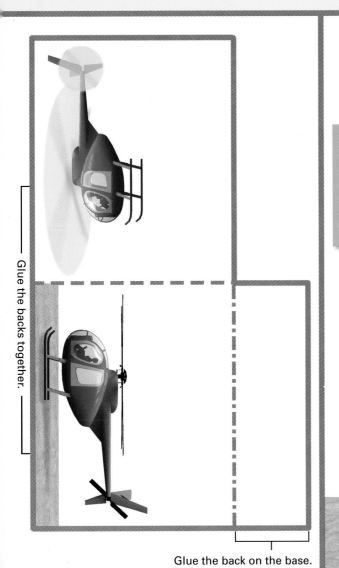

Glue the backs together.

Glue the back on the base.

## Helicopter

A helicopter can fly forwards, backwards and side to side.

# 12 Cargo Aircraft

■ Cut, fold and paste the cargo aircraft's nose, then paste the part on the base to complete. Play with the cargo aircraft to make it unload its goods.

● HOW TO CREATE AND PLAY

1. Cut along ▬▬▬▬.
   Then fold downwards along ----
   and upwards along ▬·▬·▬.

2. Glue the backs together.

3. Paste the part on the base.

4. Move the part to make the cargo airplane unload its goods.

## Cargo Aircraft

A cargo aircraft carries goods instead of people.

Glue the back on the base.

Glue the backs together.

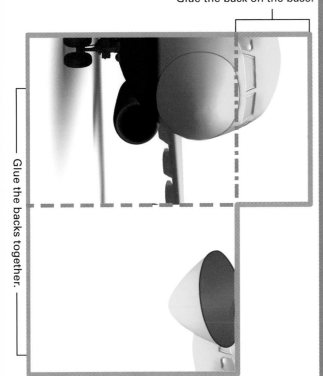

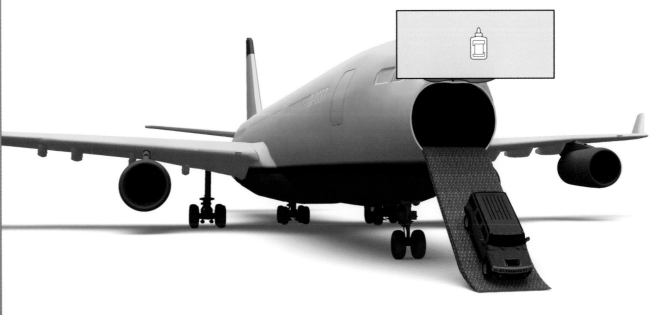

# 13 Train

■ Cut, fold and paste the doorway, then paste the part on the base to complete.
Play with the doorway to let the passengers onto the train.

● HOW TO CREATE AND PLAY

1. Cut along ▬▬▬▬.
Then fold downwards along – – – –
and upwards along – · – · – · – .

2. Glue
the backs
together.

3. Paste the part on
the base.

4. Move the part to let the
passengers onto the train.

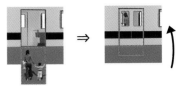

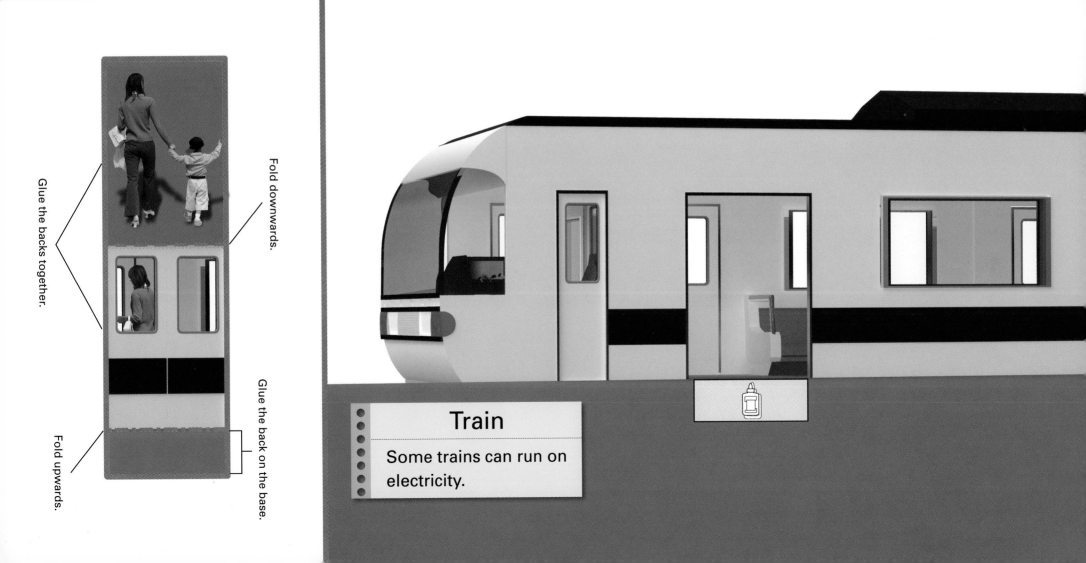

Glue the backs together.

Fold downwards.

Glue the back on the base.

Fold upwards.

## Train

Some trains can run on electricity.

# Ambulance

■ Cut, fold and paste the stretcher, then paste the part on the base to complete. Play with the stretcher to bring the patient into the hospital.

## ● HOW TO CREATE AND PLAY

1. Cut along ▬▬▬▬.
   Then fold downwards along ‑ ‑ ‑ ‑ and upwards along ‑ ‑·‑ ·‑.

2. Glue the backs together.

3. Paste the part on the base.

4. Move the part to bring the patient into the hospital.

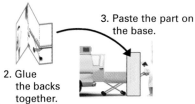

## Ambulance

An ambulance rushes injured or sick people to a hospital.

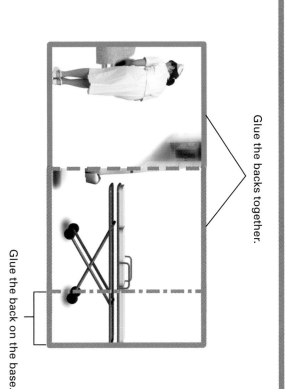

Glue the backs together.

Glue the back on the base.

# 15 Police Car

■ Cut, fold and paste the police lights, then paste the part on the base to complete. Play with the police car to make the lights flash.

## HOW TO CREATE AND PLAY

1. Cut along ▬▬▬▬.
   Then fold downwards along ‒ ‒ ‒ ‒
   and upwards along ‒ ·‒ ·‒ ·.

2. Glue the backs together.

3. Paste the part on the base.

4. Move the part to make the police car flash its lights.

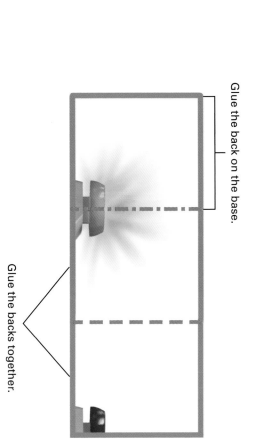

Glue the back on the base.

Glue the backs together.

## Police Car

A police car rushes through traffic by flashing its police lights and turning on its siren.

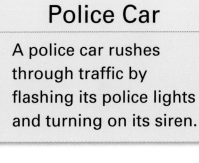

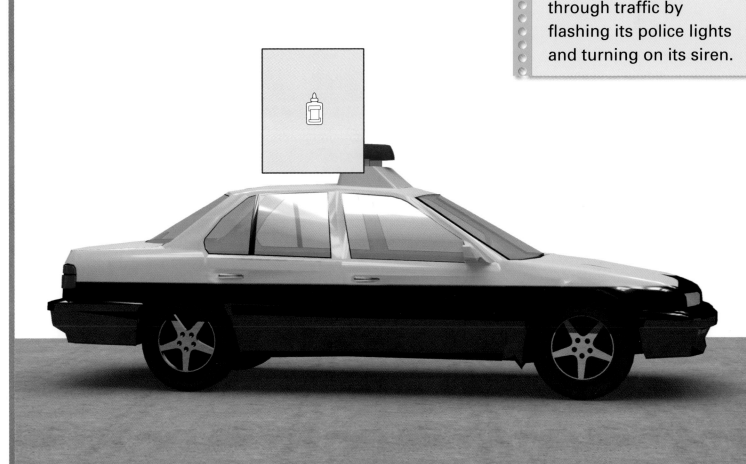

# 16 Forklift

HOW TO CREATE AND PLAY

1. Cut along ▬▬▬▬.
   Then fold downwards along ----
   and upwards along —·—·—.

2. Glue the backs together.

3. Paste the part on the base.

4. Move the part to make the forklift move the cargo up and down.

■ Cut, fold and paste the cargo, then paste the part on the base to complete. Play with the forklift to make it move the cargo up and down.

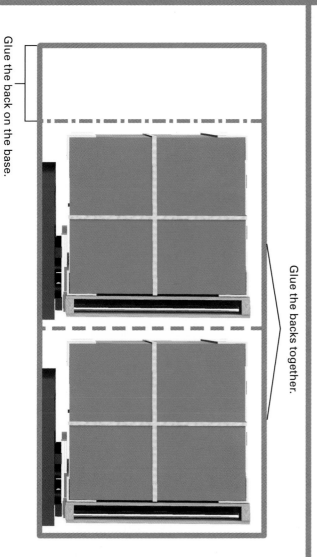

Glue the back on the base.

Glue the backs together.

## Forklift

A forklift raises and moves heavy cargo.

# Glass-Bottom Boat

■ Cut, fold and paste the bottom of the boat, then paste the part on the base to complete.  Play with the glass-bottom boat so the passengers can see the fish and plants.

● HOW TO CREATE AND PLAY

1. Cut along ▬▬▬.
   Then fold downwards along ‒ ‒ ‒ ‒
   and upwards along ▬ · ▬ · ▬ · .

2. Glue the backs together.

3. Paste the part on the base.

4. Move the part to make the glass-bottom boat show the sea.

---

Glue the back on the base.

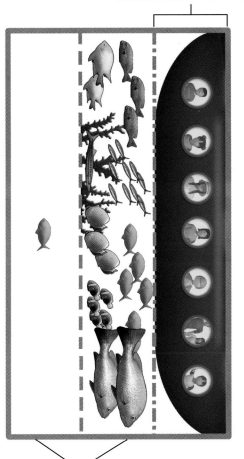

Glue the backs together.

## Glass-Bottom Boat

People can observe underwater life from the inside of a glass-bottom boat.

# 18 Car

■ Cut, fold and paste the windshield wipers, then paste the part on the base to complete. Play with the car to make the wipers wipe the windshield.

● HOW TO CREATE AND PLAY

1. Cut along ▬▬▬▬.
   Then fold upwards along ▬·▬·▬·.

2. Glue the backs together.

3. Paste the part on the base.

4. Move the part to make the wipers move back and forth.

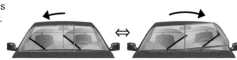

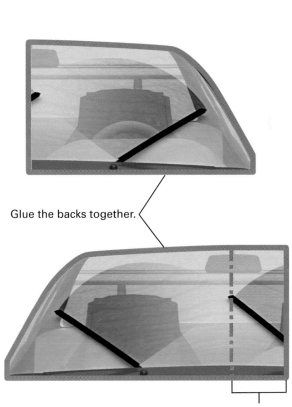

Glue the backs together.

Glue the back on the base.

## Car

A car wipes raindrops from its windshield with its wipers.

# 19 Sailboat

■ Cut, fold and paste the sailboat, then paste the part on the base to complete. Play with the sailboat to make it turn.

● HOW TO CREATE AND PLAY

1. Cut along ▬▬▬.
   Then fold downwards along – – – –
   and upwards along – ‧ – ‧ – ‧ –.

2. Glue the backs together.

3. Paste the part on the base.

4. Move the part to make the sailboat turn.

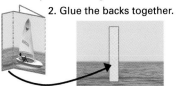
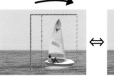

Glue the back on the base.

Glue the backs together.

## Sailboat

A sailboat travels on the sea by catching the wind in its sail.

# 20 Steam Locomotive

■ Cut, fold and paste the smoke, then paste the part on the base to complete.
Play with the steam locomotive to make the smoke rise.

## ● HOW TO CREATE AND PLAY

1. Cut along ▬▬▬.
   Then fold upwards along – ·· – ·· –.

2. Glue the backs together.

3. Paste the part on the base.

4. Move the part to make the smoke rise.

Glue the back on the base.

Glue the backs together.

## Steam Locomotive

A steam locomotive burns coal as fuel.

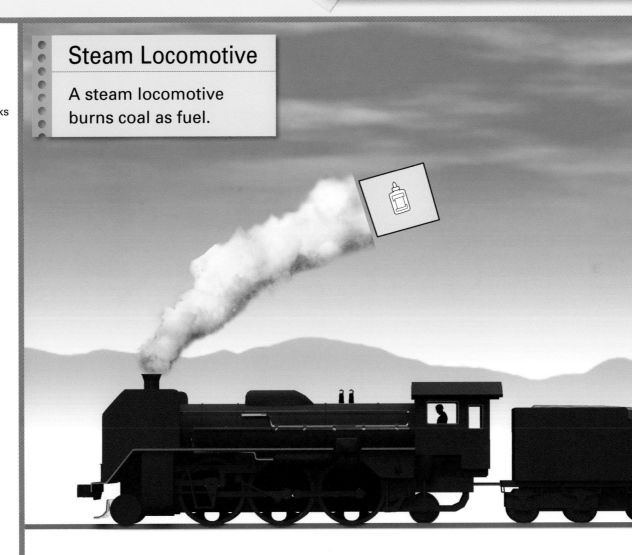

# School Bus

● HOW TO CREATE AND PLAY

1. Cut along ▬▬▬.
   Then fold downwards along ‒ ‒ ‒ ‒
   and upwards along ‒·‒·‒.

2. Glue the backs together.

3. Paste the part on the base.

4. Move the part to make the bus pick up the passenger.

■ Cut, fold and paste the school bus, then paste the part on the base to complete. Play with the school bus to make it pick up the passenger.

Glue the back on the base.

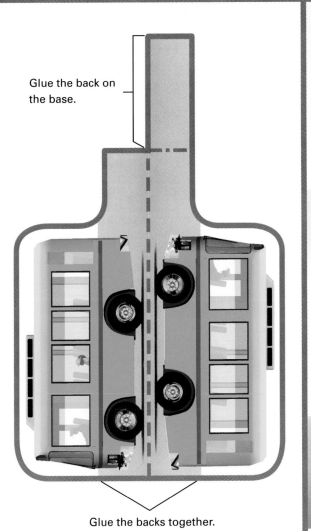

Glue the backs together.

## School Bus

A bus runs along a route to transport people.

# 22 Dump Truck

■ Cut, fold and paste the flatbed, then paste the part on the base to complete. Play with the dump truck to make it unload the rocks and sand.

● HOW TO CREATE AND PLAY

1. Cut along ▬▬▬▬.
   Then fold upwards along ▬·▬·▬·.

2. Glue the backs together.

3. Paste the part on the base.

4. Move the part to make the dump truck unload the rocks and sand.

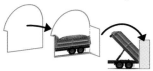

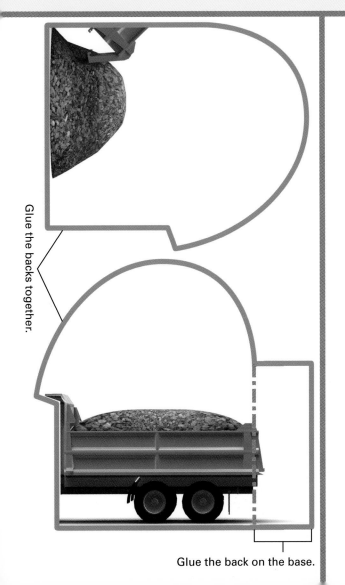

Glue the backs together.

Glue the back on the base.

## Dump Truck

A dump truck tilts its flatbed to unload rocks and sand.

# 23 Bulldozer

Cut, fold and paste the bulldozer, then paste the part on the base to complete. Play with the bulldozer to make it move.

● HOW TO CREATE AND PLAY

1. Cut along ▬▬▬.
   Then fold downwards along ▬ ▬ ▬
   and upwards along ▬ · ▬ · ▬.

2. Glue the backs together.

3. Paste the part on the base.

4. Move the part to make the bulldozer move.

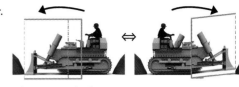

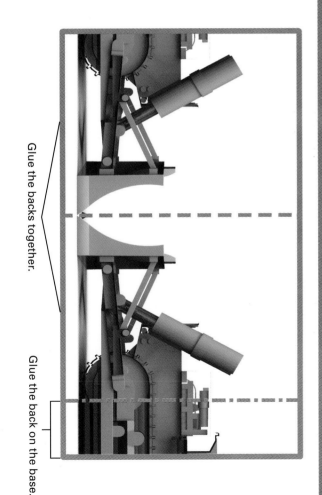

Glue the backs together.

Glue the back on the base.

## Bulldozer

A bulldozer pushes dirt and can flatten the ground.

# Hang Glider

■ Cut, fold and paste the hang glider, then paste the part on the base to complete.  Play with the hang glider to make it fly.

● HOW TO CREATE AND PLAY

1. Cut along ▬▬▬.
   Then fold upwards along ▬·▬·▬·▬.

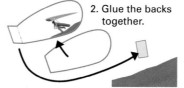

2. Glue the backs together.

4. Move the part to make the hang glider fly.

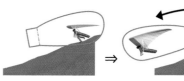

3. Paste the part on the base.

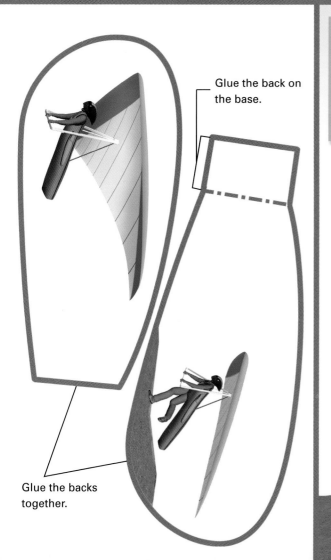

Glue the back on the base.

Glue the backs together.

## Hang Glider

A hang glider has no engine; it glides through the air by using the wind.

# 25 Cherry Picker

■ Cut, fold and paste the cherry picker, then paste the part on the base to complete. Play with the cherry picker to make it reach high.

● HOW TO CREATE AND PLAY

1. Cut along ▬▬▬.
   Then fold upwards along ▬·▬·▬·▬.

2. Glue the backs together.

3. Paste the part on the base.

4. Move the part to make the cherry picker reach high.

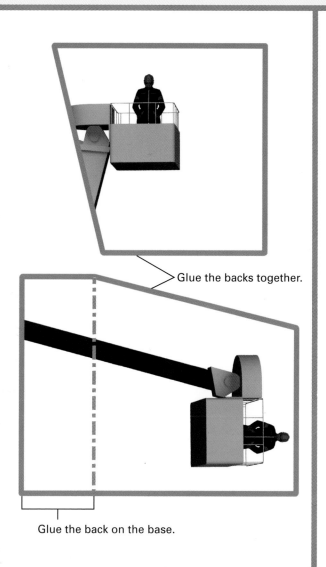

Glue the backs together.

Glue the back on the base.

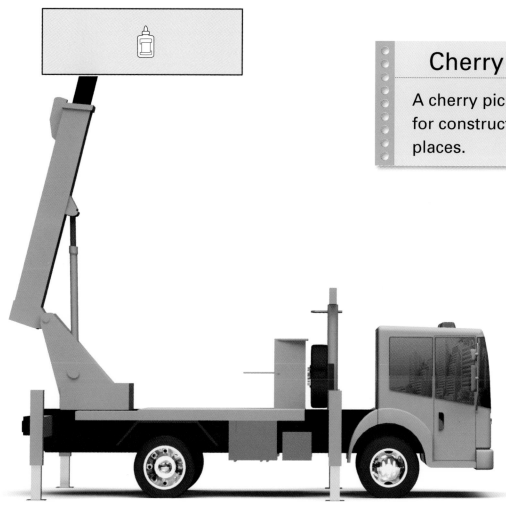

## Cherry Picker

A cherry picker is used for construction in high places.

# 26 Express Train

■ Cut, fold and paste the express train, then paste the part on the base to complete. Play with the express train to make it speed out of the tunnel.

● HOW TO CREATE AND PLAY

1. Cut along ▬▬▬▬.
   Then fold downwards along ‐ ‐ ‐ ‐
   and upwards along ‐·‐·‐· .

2. Glue the backs together.

3. Paste the part on the base.

4. Move the part to make the express train speed out of the tunnel.

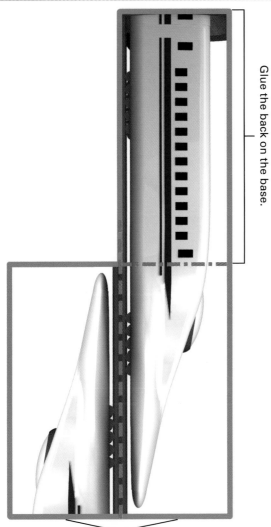

Glue the back on the base.

Glue the backs together.

## Express Train

An express train runs faster than normal trains.

# 27 Ferry

■ Cut, fold and paste the cars unloading from the ferry, then paste the part on the base to complete. Play with the ferry to make it unload the cars.

● HOW TO CREATE AND PLAY

1. Cut along ▬▬▬▬.
   Then fold downwards along ━ ━ ━ ━
   and upwards along ━ · ━ · ━ · .

2. Glue the backs together.

3. Paste the part on the base.

4. Move the part to make the ferry unload the cars.

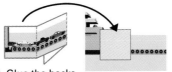

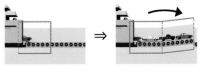

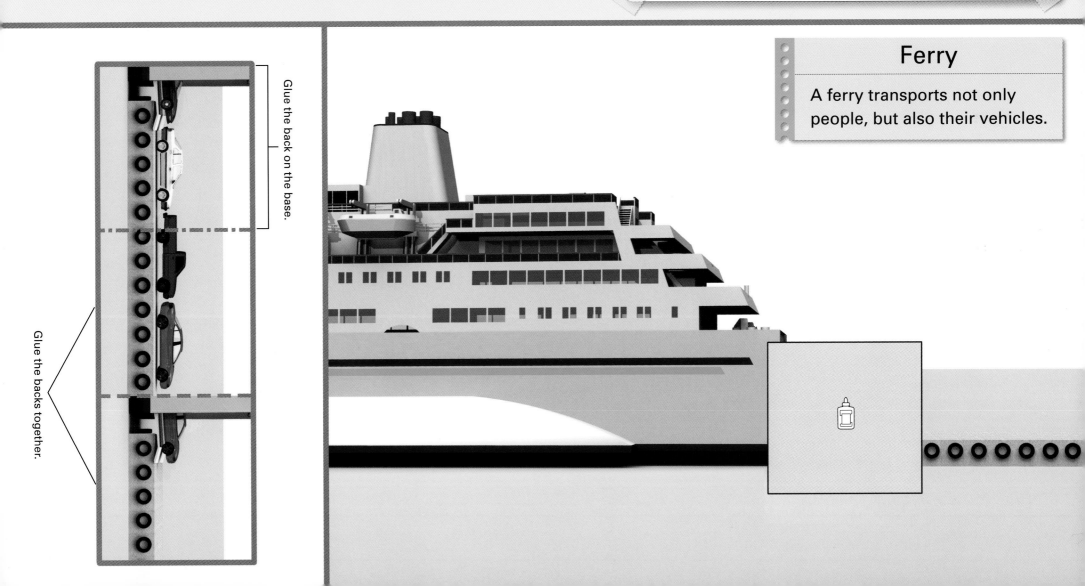

Glue the back on the base.

Glue the backs together.

## Ferry

A ferry transports not only people, but also their vehicles.

# 28 Hook and Ladder Truck

■ Cut, fold and paste the ladder, then paste the part on the base to complete. Play with the hook and ladder truck to extend the ladder.

● HOW TO CREATE AND PLAY

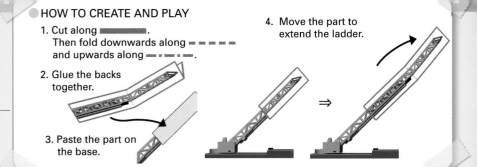

1. Cut along ▬▬▬▬▬.
   Then fold downwards along ▬ ▬ ▬ ▬
   and upwards along ▬ ▪ ▬ ▪ ▬.
2. Glue the backs together.
3. Paste the part on the base.
4. Move the part to extend the ladder.

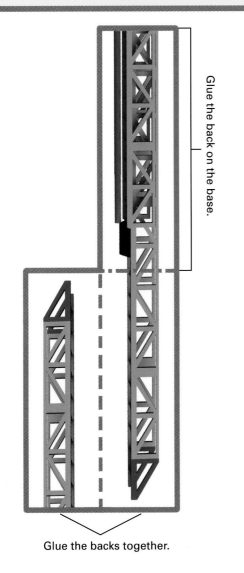

Glue the back on the base.

Glue the backs together.

## Hook and Ladder Truck

A hook and ladder truck rescues people in high places with its long ladder.

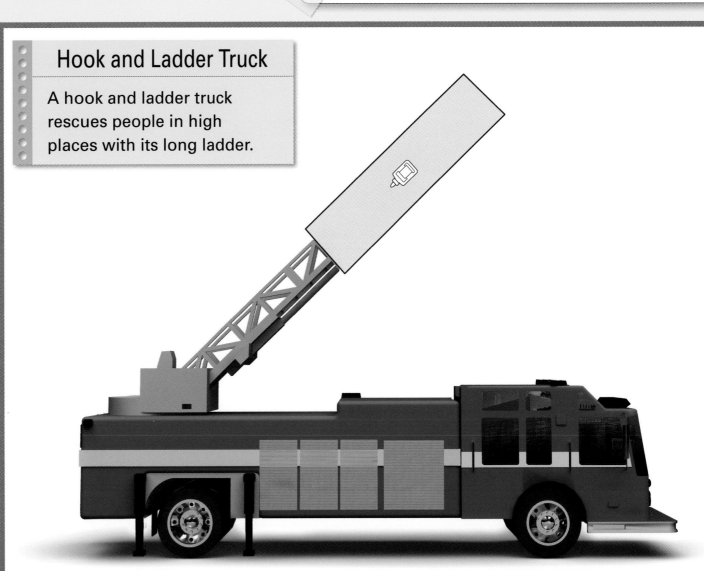

# Fire Helicopter

■ HOW TO CREATE AND PLAY

1. Cut along ▬▬▬▬.
   Then fold downwards along ----- and upwards along ▬ · ▬ · ▬ ·.

3. Move the part to make the fire helicopter put out the forest fire.

2. Paste the part on the base.

■ Cut and fold the water, then paste it on the base to complete.
Play with the fire helicopter to make it put out the forest fire.

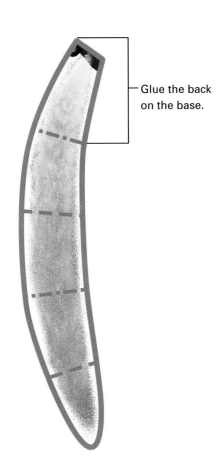

Glue the back on the base.

## Fire Helicopter

A fire helicopter puts out big fires from the air.

# 30 Auto Transporter

■ Cut, fold and paste the ramp, then paste the part on the base to complete. Play with the auto transporter to make it load the cars.

● HOW TO CREATE AND PLAY

1. Cut along ▬▬▬.
   Then fold downwards along ‑ ‑ ‑ ‑ ‑
   and upwards along ‑ ‑ · ‑ · ‑ .

2. Glue the backs together.

3. Paste the part on the base.

4. Move the part to make the transporter load the cars.

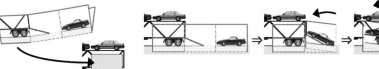

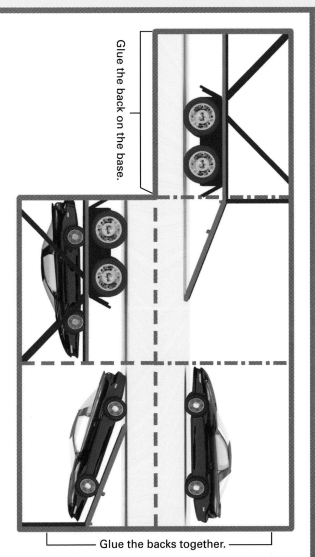

Glue the back on the base.

Glue the backs together.

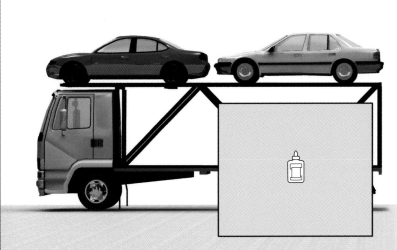

## Transporter

A transporter can load and carry many cars.

# Certificate of Achievement

_____

is hereby congratulated on completing

## Paper Playtime: Vehicles

**Presented on** _____ ,20_____

_ _ _ _ _ _ _ _ _ _ _ _ _ _ _ _ _ _ _ _ _ _

**Parent or Guardian**